Pride
and
Prejudice

Jane Austen

ai Academic Industries, Inc.
West Haven, Connecticut 06516

ISBN 0-88301-758-X

Published by
Academic Industries, Inc.
The Academic Building
Saw Mill Road
West Haven, Connecticut 06516

Printed in the United States of America

about the author

The daughter of a village preacher, Jane Austen was born in December, 1775, in the county of Hampshire, England. She received her early education at home from her father, although she was sent for a brief time to a boarding school not far away. During her spare time she enjoyed reading, country walks, and good conversation.

As one of seven children, Jane found most of her entertainment at home. Her earliest writings, in fact, were stories and plays she had created for her family's enjoyment. By the time she was twenty she had begun two novels, *Pride and Prejudice* and *Sense and Sensibility*. Among her other works, written later in her life, were *Northanger Abbey*, *Mansfield Park*, and *Emma*.

All of Jane Austen's novels deal with the manners and social life of upper-class Englishmen during the eighteenth century. Although there is little adventure in any of them, critics say they are among the most interesting works of English fiction because they present a realistic picture of family life at that time. Frequently ill during her later years, Jane Austen died in 1817 at the age of forty-two.

Pride and Prejudice

Jane Austen

Mr. Bingley

Mr. Darcy

Elizabeth Bennet

Jane Bennet

Mrs. Bennet

In England, at the time of our story, marriage was the only accepted way of life for young women without much money. This was so even if they were unhappy about it.

The Bennets had five daughters and little money. The business of Mrs. Bennet's life was to get her daughters married.

Soon Mr. Bennet called on Mr. Bingley. A few days later, Mr. Bingley visited the Bennets.

I hear there is to be a dance soon?

Yes, indeed. And you will be very welcome.

Mr. Bingley had heard of the five beautiful Bennet daughters. He did not see them, but they saw him.

I think he's handsome. What a beautiful blue coat!

And what a handsome black horse!

9

Soon after, Mrs. Bennet talked to her friend, Lady Lucas.

I invited Mr. Bingley to dinner, but he had to go to London.

Isn't he going to settle down at Netherfield?

Oh, yes. I think he went to invite guests for our dance! Twelve ladies and seven men, I heard!

Then the night of the dance arrived.

Who are those people?

Mr. Bingley's sister, Mrs. Hurst and her husband. And his unmarried sister. How nice they look!

And Mr. Darcy. He's even better looking than Mr. Bingley . . . and much richer, they say!

Mr. Bingley soon met everyone and danced every dance.

He danced with Charlotte Lucas.

He danced with Elizabeth Bennet.

He danced most of all with Jane.

There were not enough men, but Darcy danced only twice— with the Bingley ladies.

I don't think you care for this dance.

That's true. I won't dance with anyone here but you and your sister.

And he talked only with his friends.

Come, Darcy, you must dance! There are so many nice girls here!

No indeed! I would hate it!

You are dancing with the only beautiful girl in the room!

She is the *most* beautiful girl I have ever seen! But I want you to meet her sister, who is also very pretty.

The young lady over there?

Exactly!

Not pretty enough for *me*! You are wasting your time!

You are hopeless!

Hearing what Darcy had said, Elizabeth was both angry and amused.

After the dance, Jane and Elizabeth talked about what had happened.

I admire Mr. Bingley very much! He is smart, lively, and very funny!

And handsome, too!

I was surprised that he asked me to dance so often! I did not expect such a compliment.

And why not? He could not help seeing that you were five times prettier than anyone else!

Dear Lizzy!

And he *is* very nice—even though you find *everyone* good and never speak badly of anyone!

And do you like his sisters too? *I* didn't like them at all!

Not at first, but they are very charming to talk with.

The Lucases were neighbors and close friends of the Bennets. Sir William had been knighted after making his money in selling. The morning after the dance. . . .

I suppose you're off to the Bennets' house?

Yes, indeed . . . to talk about the dance!

I can't wait to hear what Lizzy has to say.

Charlotte, the oldest Lucas daughter, was Elizabeth Bennet's good friend.

And after they arrived. . . .

You began the night well, Charlotte. You were Mr. Bingley's first choice!

But he liked his second choice better!

Oh, you mean Jane! Well, he *was* heard calling her the prettiest girl in the room. We'll see what comes of it.

Oh, Mother!

The subject changed to Mr. Darcy.

I never saw such a rude man! He refused to dance with Elizabeth!

Still—he is good looking and rich!

He almost has a *right* to be proud.

True! And I could easily forgive *his* pride if he had not hurt mine!

Soon the Bennet ladies and the Bingley ladies visited each other. And Mr. Bingley and Jane met at several evening parties.

Everyone could see that Mr. Bingley was falling in love.

Jane left on horseback. Soon after, it rained.

Jane will be wet!

My plan *was* good! They'll have to keep her overnight!

After a stormy night, a servant brought a note from Jane.

Jane is ill with a sore throat and a headache. The Bingleys want her to stay there until she is better.

What a good idea!

If your daughter dies, you will be happy knowing that it was your plan to chase Mr. Bingley.

People don't die of little colds! I would go to see her if I could use the coach.

I will go anyway, even if I must walk.

How silly, in all this mud! You will be so dirty when you get there!

That doesn't matter. I want to see Jane.

After a three-mile walk across the fields, Elizabeth arrived at Netherfield.

I *am* dirty. They'll have to understand!

She was brought into the breakfast room.

You *walked* here? In such weather?

So early in the day? By yourself?

Yes, indeed. I was worried about Jane.

Good for you!

18

Elizabeth was taken up to Jane's room. She found her with a headache, a fever, and a sore throat.

Lizzy! I am so glad to see you! Everyone here has been so kind!

My dear, you *should* be treated well.

Elizabeth stayed with Jane during the day. Late in the afternoon, she prepared to leave.

Dear Jane, I must start for home.

Oh, Lizzy! I wish you could stay with me!

Well, of course . . . if that is what dear Jane wants . . . you must stay.

A servant went to the Bennet house to bring back clothes for Elizabeth. Meanwhile, dinner was served.

I admire your sister so much! I hope she'll feel better soon!

You and your sisters have cared for her so kindly!

When dinner was over, Elizabeth returned at once to Jane's room. As soon as she left, the ladies began to talk about her.

Well! How rude she is! No small talk, no style, no taste. . . .

And the way she looked this morning! Her petticoat was covered with mud. . . .

I thought she looked very well. And she showed a pleasing love for her sister!

And you, Mr. Darcy? I am sure you noticed her dirty petticoat?

Not at all. But I noticed her very pretty eyes!

Jane Bennet is a dear, sweet girl. I wish she could marry someone rich. But with her family, there's not a chance.

Her mother and father have no money. And her uncle is a lawyer!

It doesn't make her less beautiful!

Each night after Jane was asleep, Elizabeth went down to the living room just to be nice.

Mr. Bingley was always very concerned.

She is better? I do hope so!

There is nothing to worry about.

Meanwhile, Darcy was falling in love with Elizabeth.

Never have I been so charmed by a woman! But her lowly family will keep me safe from marrying her.

Miss Bingley hoped to marry Darcy herself.

He really finds her pretty! I will do all I can to change *that!*

In a few days Jane felt much better. On Sunday she wanted to go home with Elizabeth.

How foolish of you to come home! I hope you don't catch cold again!

No, Mama, I am quite well.

I am glad to see you both!

Mrs. Bennet's sister, married to Mr. Philips, lived nearby in Meryton. The girls often visited their aunt.

The youngest Bennet daughters always learned the news first.

Soldiers have arrived here in Meryton. They will stay for the winter! Isn't that exciting?

We watch the officers from aunt's windows. They are so handsome!

At breakfast the next day, Mr. Bennet read a letter from his cousin, William Collins. According to the law, Mr. Collins would someday inherit all of Mr. Bennet's money.

This was because Mr. Bennet had no sons.

This is from the man who can put all of you out of this house when I am dead!

That terrible man!

It is a cruel thing! Why should he write to you? We don't even know him!

He is sorry about the fight between our families. He would like to meet us and make friends!

He has just become a minister and has been given a church in Kent by Lady Catherine de Bourgh.

"I am sorry if I have hurt your daughters," he writes, "and I would like to make it up to them."

Well! That makes sense!

He wanted to come this afternoon for a visit. I wrote him to come!

I'm glad he's sorry.

I wonder what he's like. He sounds very odd.

23

Mr. Collins arrived at four o'clock. He was welcomed by the whole family.

I have heard about your beautiful daughters, and it is true! I am sure you will see them married to the right men soon!

You are very kind.

At dinner he talked much of his patroness, Lady Catherine de Bourgh.

Many people think she's proud, but she has been very kind to me. Thanks to her, I have a good house and money. She thinks I should marry soon!

The next morning. . . .

It was my hope to marry one of your lovely daughters. Perhaps this will make up for our past troubles.

I see! How very nice!

My oldest, Jane, is likely to be engaged soon!

Then I will think about Miss Elizabeth!

Mrs. Bennet could hardly believe her good luck. Two daughters almost engaged!

That afternoon the girls and Mr. Collins walked to Meryton.

Look! Mr. Denny and a stranger!

How handsome he is! If he were a soldier he would be just right!

Soon the two groups met.

BONNETS

I would like you to meet Mr. Wickham. He is going to be a soldier!

As they talked, two horsemen drew near.

Miss Bennet! I was just on my way to ask about your health!

How good of you! I am well, as you can see.

25

Suddenly . . .

What is it? One man grows pale, the other red . . . how strange!

Darcy and Wickham barely spoke. Then Darcy rode on.

Did you notice? They acted so strangely!

No, tell me!

The next night the Philipses gave a party. The Bennet girls were there. So were many army officers.

Mr. Wickham in his uniform is far more handsome than the rest of them!

Which of us will he choose?

Card tables were set up. Some of the guests played whist. But Mr. Wickham talked to Elizabeth.

Were you surprised at the way I acted when I met Darcy yesterday? Do you know him well?

Well enough! I find him very rude.

In this neighborhood everyone dislikes the way he acts!

I am surprised! Most people like Darcy because he is rich and important.

We grew up together. My father worked for his. In his will, Darcy's father left me the best church that he had. I would have become a minister.

But when the job was open, Darcy gave it to someone else. So I am a soldier now.

How wicked! Why would he do such a thing?

He *really* dislikes me! Maybe it is because his father was very fond of me.

What kind of girl is his sister?

Just like her brother! When she was a child, we were friends. Now she is fifteen or sixteen—pretty, important, and she means nothing to me!

I wonder how Darcy and Mr. Bingley can be good friends. Bingley is so kind!

The card game ended. Mr. Collins stood next to Elizabeth.

Did you win?

Not at all. I lost every point!

I am so sorry you lost your money!

Please don't worry! Thanks to Lady Catherine de Bourgh, five shillings isn't much money to me!

Is your family friendly with Lady Catherine de Bourgh?

Not at all! She has just made my cousin the minister of a church on her land.

She is Mr. Darcy's aunt! Her daughter will be very rich, and she just might marry Darcy.

That will not make Miss Bingley happy!

The party was over and the guests went home. The next day, the Bennets had visitors.

The date for our party at Netherfield is next Tuesday!

Will you come? We haven't seen you for days!

How kind of you to invite us!

We're invited? And the officers will be there? Oh, joy!

On the night of the party, Elizabeth wanted to dance with Wickham. But Collins walked up first.

Come, my dear cousin! I *must* have the first two dances!

But I . . . well . . . of course, thank you.

And later. . . .

Where is that wonderful Mr. Wickham tonight?

He is away on business. Perhaps his business would not have kept him away if a certain man were not here!

29

Elizabeth could see that Mr. Collins was looking at her. And the next day. . . .

I hope you will give your consent when I ask your daughter to marry me.

I am sure that Lizzy will be very happy. Come, Kitty, I want you upstairs!

No, don't go, please!

But Mrs. Bennet and Kitty hurried away.

Almost as soon as I entered the house I wanted to marry you. But first I will give you my reasons.

Every minister should be married.

It is the wish of my patroness, Lady Catherine de Bourgh.

And since I will inherit your father's money, I want to choose my wife from among his daughters.

He talked on and on. At last Elizabeth was able to speak.

Wait! Thank you for asking me to marry you. But I cannot accept!

Oh, yes, I know that young ladies feel they must refuse at least once or twice! I will ask again soon.

I *cannot* marry you, now or ever! I don't love you!

I am sure that when your parents agree to our marriage, you will accept!

Elizabeth left the room. Later, Mrs. Bennet talked to her husband.

Mr. Bennet, you must come and make Lizzy marry Mr. Collins! She vows she will not accept him!

And what can I do about it?

Speak to her! Tell her that she *must* marry him! Or I will never talk to her again!

I'll try. Send for Elizabeth.

Elizabeth came to the reading room.

Elizabeth, you have a hard choice. Your mother will never talk to you again unless you marry Mr. Collins. And I will never talk to you again if you *do*!

Mrs. Bennet was upset with Mr. Bennet and Elizabeth. When Charlotte Lucas came to visit, she heard all about it.

I am glad you have come! Mr. Collins wants to marry Lizzy.

And she has refused him!

So you've heard the news! Please tell Lizzy to change her mind. Nobody is on my side in this!

She always wants to have her own way! But if you refuse every offer and never get a husband, who will take care of you when your father is dead?

Then Mr. Collins himself entered.

Now I want all of you to be quiet and let Mr. Collins and me have a talk.

The way your daughter acts has made me wish to take back my offer of marriage.

Oh, Mr. Collins!

After talking to Mrs. Bennet, he turned to Charlotte.

My dear Miss Lucas, how is your health? And are your father and mother well?

Thank you, we are all well.

That afternoon a letter came for Jane. When she and Elizabeth were alone, she opened it.

It is from Caroline Bingley. The Bingleys and the Darcys have returned to London, and she says they don't want to come back!

Perhaps *she* doesn't want her brother to return. *He* may not feel that way!

She writes that they expect to see much of Darcy's sister, Georgiana, this winter.

Caroline says she is beautiful, and that Charles thinks she is wonderful.

Their family wants and expects them to be engaged.

I believe she knows my feelings for Charles. She is warning me that there is no hope for us.

That's silly! She sees that Charles is in love with you. We are not rich enough or important enough for *her*!

She wants Miss Darcy for her brother, and Darcy for herself! But I don't think that she can make Charles marry Miss Darcy instead of you!

I don't believe Caroline would lie to me.

I am sure that Charles will return to you, dear sister!

But Elizabeth was wrong. It would be many months before Bingley returned.

The next morning Mr. Collins hurried to Lucas Lodge.

If I can talk with Miss Lucas alone, I will ask her to marry me!

Charlotte saw him coming.

It's Mr. Collins! I must hurry out and meet him.

In a short time they were making plans.

My dear Miss Charlotte, name the day that will make me a happy man!

Let us talk with my parents.

The next day Mr. Collins left for home. Charlotte, who was very friendly with Elizabeth, went to tell her the news.

You? Engaged to Mr. Collins? My dear Charlotte, impossible!

Did you think he wouldn't marry anyone else because he didn't get you?

I am twenty-seven years old. I don't care about love. All I ask for is a nice home.

I believe my chances of happiness with Mr. Collins are good.

My dear Charlotte, I wish you all the happiness in the world!

36

Mrs. Bennet was very upset when she heard the news about Charlotte.

To think that I must live to see the day when *Charlotte Lucas* will own my home!

Cheer up, my dear. Perhaps *I* may be the last to die.

It's all your fault, Elizabeth. You are a wicked, selfish girl!

It would be a week before Mrs. Bennet could see Elizabeth without getting angry. And it would be a month before she could speak to the Lucases without being rude.

It was lucky that Mrs. Bennet's brother and his wife, the Gardiners, came to spend Christmas with her.

Can you believe it? *Two* of my girls were almost engaged, but now there is no hope!

I *am* sorry!

I don't blame Jane. She would have married Mr. Bingley if she could!

Mother!

But Lizzy! She might have been Mr. Collins' wife. But now Lady Lucas will have a married daughter before I do!

Mrs. Gardiner and the two girls were good friends. So the older woman spoke to Elizabeth.

I am sorry for Jane. Would she come to London with us for a visit?

It would be good for her to get away!

She would not have to see young Bingley unless he came to see her!

Don't worry! Mr. Darcy would never allow him to visit Jane!

But doesn't Jane still write letters to Caroline Bingley? *She* will tell him that Jane is there.

I don't think so.

Many dances took place while the Gardiners were visiting.

Who is the young man giving so much attention to Elizabeth?

That's Mr. Wickham! Isn't he handsome?

After the dance, Mrs. Gardiner spoke to Lizzy.

My dear, Wickham is very handsome, but he doesn't have any money! I think you are too smart for that!

For what? To fall in love with a young man too poor to marry me?

I know it would not be wise. But he is one of the nicest men I know.

But soon Wickham was thinking of someone else.

Wickham is going out with Miss King. She has just inherited some money!

I never cared for him anyway.

But Miss King is *ugly!*

I hear she is a very nice girl. And *handsome* young men must have something to live on as well as plain ones!

Not long afterward, Jane went to London with the Gardiners. The Collins-Lucas wedding day drew near. Charlotte paid a farewell visit to her friend Elizabeth.

I expect to hear from you often, Elizabeth.

You will!

Promise me you'll come and visit us?

Yes, of course.

My father and Maria are coming to visit in March. Please come with them! I'd love to have you!

Soon, the wedding took place. The happy couple went from the church door directly to Kent.

After two quiet months, Elizabeth went with the Lucases for a visit to Charlotte's new home.

This must be the house!

Yes, there they are!

First the guests were welcomed. Then Charlotte took them to see all the rooms of the house and the land around it.

There is Rosings, Lady Catherine de Bourgh's country home. Isn't it beautiful!

You will see Lady de Bourgh on Sunday at church, Miss Elizabeth.

I am sure she will invite you and Maria to many events while you are here.

She is very nice to us. We eat at Rosings twice a week, and she always has her coach bring us home!

The next day Elizabeth heard a great deal of talking.

Quick! Hurry down to the dining room. There is something I want you to see!

The girls looked through the dining room window.

It is Miss de Bourgh! I didn't think she would be so small and thin.

She is very rude to keep Charlotte out in all this wind.

She looks sickly and mean. She will make a good wife for Mr. Darcy!

The old lady is Mrs. Jenkinson, who lives with them.

The ladies drove on. Mr. Collins explained their visit.

How very lucky for you! Lady Catherine has invited our whole group to dine with her tomorrow!

The dinner was as good as Mr. Collins had promised. Lady Catherine did most of the talking.

What? Four sisters at home, and no governess? If I had known your mother, I would have told her to hire one!

I'm sure you would!

Soon Sir William went home, leaving Maria and Elizabeth for a longer visit. And there were visitors at Rosings too.

Lady Catherine's nephews are visiting her—Mr. Darcy and Colonel Fitzwilliam.

Oh, yes. We know Mr. Darcy.

Yes, indeed!

The girls were asked to come to Rosings. Colonel Fitzwilliam liked Elizabeth very much.

What are you saying to Miss Bennet, Fitzwilliam? Let me hear it!

We are talking about music. Miss Bennet will play the piano for me.

Elizabeth began to play. Soon Darcy moved to face her.

You want to scare me, Mr. Darcy, but I won't let you!

You don't believe that! I think you just enjoy saying things like that.

From then on, Fitzwilliam and Darcy often visited the Collins' home.

I can't understand it! Colonel Fitzwilliam laughs and talks and enjoys himself. But why does Darcy come?

He only sits and stares—and mostly at you, Elizabeth! I almost believe he's in love with you!

No chance of that! We don't agree about anything!

Yet one day, Darcy came to see Elizabeth when she was alone.

I have fought my feelings, but I can't get rid of them. I must tell you how much I love you!

You are not the wife I would have chosen. We are not suited for each other—but my feelings for you are so strong that I hope you will marry me.

You have not said one nice thing about me. Why don't you forget the whole thing!

Is that all you have to say to me?

I have every reason to think badly of you! Would I accept the man who has spoiled the happiness of my dear sister? Can you deny it?

No! And I am sorry about it.

Wickham is poor. He's had problems, and it's all because of you!

So that is what you think. Thank you for explaining it to me!

I've had enough! Forgive me for taking up your time.

Elizabeth was too surprised and upset to think of anything else. And when she got up the next morning, she was still upset.

She went out, hoping a walk would calm her feelings. Outside, she saw Darcy again.

I have been waiting for you. Will you read this letter?

Handing it to her, Darcy quickly walked away.

"Do not be afraid—I will not repeat the things I said yesterday, but I *had* to write this letter. After reading it, you may understand things a little better.

It is true that I joined Bingley's sisters in trying to make him forget Jane.

I told Bingley that Jane didn't love him. And from what I can see, I don't think she does."

It's true—I told Jane that she hid her feelings *too well*!

"As for Wickham, I can only tell you of the way he fooled my father and the way he treated my sister and me. Why don't you speak to Colonel Fitzwilliam who also knows the truth."

Wickham did not *want* to become a minister. So Darcy gave him a great deal of money to study law. Instead, Wickham wasted it. Can this be true?

Then last summer, Wickham made plans with the lady who took care of Darcy's fifteen-year-old sister. He won Georgiana's love and asked her to run away with him. His reason for this was her money!

"At the last moment, she decided not to go through with it. Georgiana told me everything. Wickham quickly left the town. We didn't see him for a long time after that."

For two hours, Elizabeth walked. She could not believe it all. But still. . . .

I knew nothing about Wickham except that he said nice things to me. Darcy hurt my feelings. So I didn't like Darcy, and I believed everything Wickham said!

At last Elizabeth returned to the house.

Darcy and Fitzwilliam called to say goodbye. They leave tomorrow. It is too bad you missed them!

Then the time came for Elizabeth and Maria to leave. Jane joined them in London, and together they went home.

You look well, Jane!

I am glad you are back, Lizzy.

Once again the family was together.

Bad news! The soldiers are leaving Meryton in two weeks! But there's good news too—about a person we all like!

Mary King has moved to her uncle's house in Liverpool—so Wickham is safe from marrying her!

And Mary King is safe from *him*.

We must go to see Pemberley! It's a fine house, and the land around it is so beautiful!

Oh, dear!

Elizabeth was upset. Suppose they met Darcy? What would he think?

But at the inn she found out that the Darcys were away. So the next morning they went to Pemberley.

What a beautiful place!

A housekeeper showed them through the main rooms.

That's Mr. Darcy. I've known him since he was four years old, and he's always been very good to me!

I'm glad to hear that!

Any one of his servants will say the same!

51

A gardener was about to show them the grounds when suddenly....

Mr. Darcy! We thought you were not here!

I just arrived. I rode ahead of everyone else.

May I meet your friends?

Yes, of course.

Soon Darcy was showing them through the beautiful grounds.

If you are a fisherman, please fish here whenever you want!

That's very kind!

The time had come to leave.

Bingley, his sisters, and my sister Georgiana will arrive here tomorrow. May I bring her to meet you during your stay?

Yes, please do!

As they drove home, Elizabeth didn't know what to think. What did it all mean? Darcy was like a different man!

The next day, Darcy arrived.

Please meet my sister, Georgiana.

How do you do!

Elizabeth soon knew that Georgiana was not proud, but only very shy!

Soon after that, Bingley arrived.

Miss Elizabeth! It has been more than eight months since I've seen any of your family! Are *all* your sisters well and still living at home?

If Bingley had counted the months since he last saw Jane, maybe he still loved her!

The visitors were asked to dine at Pemberley the next evening. And Elizabeth thought of Darcy most of the night.

I thought he would be my enemy. But it seems he has forgiven me for saying all of those mean things.

The next morning . . .

Won't you come for a walk?

No, here's a letter from Jane. I want to read the news from home!

Elizabeth grew upset as she read.

It can't be true! What shall I do!

Then Darcy entered the room.

Oh, my! What is the matter?

Excuse me. I must find my uncle at once!

The servant will find him. Let me get you a glass of wine!

No, I am all right. I've just read a letter from Jane with terrible news.

My youngest sister, Lydia, has run away with Wickham! *You* know him! She has no money to make him want to marry her!

I might have stopped it if I had told my family what I knew about him!

I am so sorry. Are you *sure* about this?

Oh, yes! They left Brighton together secretly on Sunday night. They've been traced almost to London. My father has gone there, and Jane asks for my uncle's help.

We will start for home at once.

I wish I could help! I will tell my sister you've been called away, but I won't tell her why.

The Gardiners returned to the house. The suitcases were packed quickly. Soon they were on their way home.

Maybe they *are* married! I cannot believe Wickham would be so cruel to Lydia!

Jane says Wickham's friend believes Wickham never wanted to marry her. He ran away because he owes people large amounts of money from gambling!

By the next day, Elizabeth and the Gardiners were in Longbourn.

Is there any news, Jane?

No. Father is in London and will not write again until there *is* news.

I will join him there tomorrow!

The next day Mr. Gardiner left for London. Two days later, a letter came from him.

They've been everywhere! There is not one sign of Lydia. Mr. Gardiner will send your father home and will carry on the search himself.

My poor Lydia!

Mr. Bennet returned home. Soon after, a letter arrived.

Oh, Papa! Is it good news or bad?

I hardly know yet myself, but they are found! Please read it aloud.

"They are not married, but they soon will be if you will give Lydia her equal share of your daughters' money. Wickham is better off than we thought."

"Lydia comes to stay with us today. She will be married in this house, if you agree."

Oh, thank goodness!

You will agree? They ask only for the money Lydia is supposed to have!

Yes, of course. But how much did your uncle spend to make this happen? How will I ever repay him?

You're right! Wickham would *never* marry Lydia for the small amount that is coming to her.

The money he owes will be paid, but he couldn't marry her for less than 10,000 pounds!

The wedding took place at the Gardiners' home. Then the happy couple traveled to Longbourn.

Dear Lydia! Married at sixteen—and to this nice Mr. Wickham.

My sisters must wish they were in my place!

After listening to Lydia, Elizabeth kept her thoughts to herself.

I've come to love Darcy more than any man in the world. But he would *never* have Wickham as a brother-in-law. I must give up hope!

On the day of the wedding I was so worried. My uncle was to give me away, but he was called out on business at the last minute!

He came back in time. But Mr. Darcy would have done just as well. He was with Wickham.

Darcy?

I forgot! Darcy was a secret!

Then don't say another word about it!

Later, Elizabeth wrote to her aunt.

What was Darcy doing there? He has nothing to do with *our* family. You *must* tell me!

Quickly an answer came.

My aunt writes that it was *Darcy* who went to London, found Wickham and Lydia, paid what Wickham owed, and showed him it was best to marry Lydia!

"He blamed himself that the *real* Wickham was not better known. *I* think he had another reason."

Soon Lydia and Wickham left for the army post. And other visitors arrived.

Mr. Bingley is here again for hunting. Darcy is with him!

Bingley and Darcy came in. Soon Bingley was seated next to Jane.

I have missed seeing you!

Bingley visited often after that. Soon Elizabeth knew how he felt about Jane.

Oh! Excuse me!

We are going to be married! I am so happy!

I know you'll agree that Jane's the most wonderful girl in the world!

A few days later, a coach stopped at the Bennets' house.

Lady Catherine!

This is not just a friendly visit! I've come about a terrible report I've heard!

I've heard you are to marry my nephew, Mr. Darcy! That's impossible! I want him to marry my daughter!

If that is your only reason for not wanting us together—it is not enough to keep me from accepting him.

You must not become engaged to him!

I will make no such promise!

Lady Catherine drove away angrily. Soon after, Darcy appeared.

My feelings toward you have not changed since last April. May I hope that yours toward me *have* changed?

Yes, they *have* changed—very much!

Elizabeth! It will make me the happiest man in the world if you will marry me.

Later that day . . .

We owe everything to Lady Catherine. When she told me you wouldn't promise not to marry me, it gave me hope again!

So the day came when a happy Mrs. Bennet saw her two oldest daughters married to the right men.

Georgiana loved her new sister-in-law dearly. Jane and Bingley moved to a country home near Pemberley. Only Lady Catherine was angry, and even she finally gave in and made friends!

THE END

COMPLETE LIST OF POCKET CLASSICS AVAILABLE

CLASSICS

C 1 Black Beauty
C 2 The Call of the Wild
C 3 Dr. Jekyll and Mr. Hyde
C 4 Dracula
C 5 Frankenstein
C 6 Huckleberry Finn
C 7 Moby Dick
C 8 The Red Badge of Courage
C 9 The Time Machine
C10 Tom Sawyer
C11 Treasure Island
C12 20,000 Leagues Under the Sea
C13 The Great Adventures of Sherlock Holmes
C14 Gulliver's Travels
C15 The Hunchback of Notre Dame
C16 The Invisible Man
C17 Journey to the Center of the Earth
C18 Kidnapped
C19 The Mysterious Island
C20 The Scarlet Letter
C21 The Story of My Life
C22 A Tale of Two Cities
C23 The Three Musketeers
C24 The War of the Worlds
C25 Around the World in Eighty Days
C26 Captains Courageous
C27 A Connecticut Yankee in King Arthur's Court
C28 The Hound of the Baskervilles
C29 The House of the Seven Gables
C30 Jane Eyre
C31 The Last of the Mohicans
C32 The Best of O. Henry
C33 The Best of Poe
C34 Two Years Before the Mast
C35 White Fang
C36 Wuthering Heights
C37 Ben Hur
C38 A Christmas Carol
C39 The Food of the Gods
C40 Ivanhoe
C41 The Man in the Iron Mask
C42 The Prince and the Pauper
C43 The Prisoner of Zenda
C44 The Return of the Native
C45 Robinson Crusoe
C46 The Scarlet Pimpernel

COMPLETE LIST OF POCKET CLASSICS AVAILABLE
(cont'd)

C47 The Sea Wolf
C48 The Swiss Family Robinson
C49 Billy Budd
C50 Crime and Punishment
C51 Don Quixote
C52 Great Expectations
C53 Heidi
C54 The Illiad
C55 Lord Jim
C56 The Mutiny on Board H.M.S. Bounty
C57 The Odyssey
C58 Oliver Twist
C59 Pride and Prejudice
C60 The Turn of the Screw

SHAKESPEARE

S 1 As You Like It
S 2 Hamlet
S 3 Julius Caesar
S 4 King Lear
S 5 Macbeth
S 6 The Merchant of Venice
S 7 A Midsummer Night's Dream
S 8 Othello
S 9 Romeo and Juliet
S10 The Taming of the Shrew
S11 The Tempest
S12 Twelfth Night